Chinese Origami for Children

Fold Zodiac Animals, Festival Decorations and Other Creations

Hu Yue & Lin Xin

Better Link Press

Text and Illustrations: Hu Yue, Lin Xin
Translation: Kitty Lau

Assistant Editor: Cao Yue
Editor: Wu Yuezhou
Editorial Director: Zhang Yicong

Senior Consultants: Sun Yong, Wu Ying, Yang Xinci
Managing Director and Publisher: Wang Youbu

ISBN: 978-1-60220-993-0

Address any comments about *Chinese Origami for Children* to:

Better Link Press
99 Park Ave
New York, NY 10016
USA

or

Shanghai Press and Publishing Development Company, Ltd.
F 7 Donghu Road, Shanghai, China (200031)
Email: comments_betterlinkpress@hotmail.com

Printed in China by Shenzhen Donnelley Printing Co., Ltd.

3   5   7   9   10   8   6   4   2

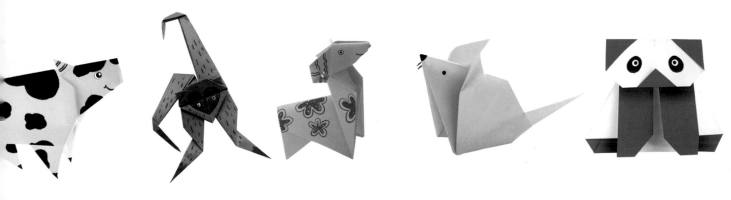

Contents

Tools and Materials 6

Getting to know Lines and Arrows 7

The Chinese Zodiac 8

1. Rat 10
2. Ox 12
3. Tiger 14
4. Rabbit 15
5. Dragon 16
6. Snake 18
7. Horse 19
8. Ram 22
9. Monkey 25
10. Rooster 28
11. Dog 30
12. Pig 33

Festivals 34

1. Carp 36
2. Lion Head 38
3. Dragon Boat 41
4. Flower Basket 44
5. Tie 47

Blessings 48

1. Butterfly 50
2. Lotus 53
3. Bottle Gourd 56
4. Longevity Peach 58

Chinese Style 60

1. *Fenghuang* 62
2. Giant Panda 66
3. Pagoda 70

A piece of paper can be transformed into different animals, plants and utensils through folding. Don't you feel like that you are a magician? This book introduces you the twelve animals of the Chinese Zodiac, as well as the celebrations of the traditional festivals. Go get a piece of paper and learn to be a magician.

Getting to Know Lines and Arrows

White side: back side of the paper.

Color side: front side of the paper.

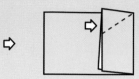

Open-headed arrow/squash fold: push to open.

 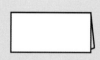

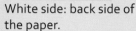

Dotted-dashed line/mountain fold: fold to the back.

Zigzag arrow/pleat fold: fold twice.

 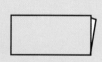

Dashed line/valley fold: fold to the front.

Curved arrow/reverse fold: push in and mountain fold along the line.

Two-headed arrow/mark fold: fold and unfold to form a crease.

Tow curved arrows/outside reverse fold: valley fold and flip outwards along the line.

Looped arrow: flip to the right 180° or flip down 180°.

Rotate 45° or 90° following the arrows.

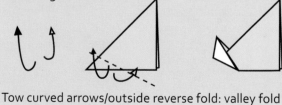

Scissors and dashed line: cut along the dashed line.

7

The Chinese Zodiac

Once upon a time, the Jade Emperor commanded all the animals to come celebrate his birthday. He put them on duty every twelve year according to the order of arrival. Later on, rat, ox, tiger, rabbit, dragon, snake, horse, ram, monkey, rooster, dog, and pig were promoted to be the twelve animals of the zodiac and represent different years on a twelve-year cycle.

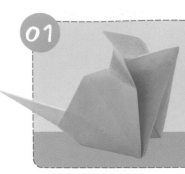

01 Rat

Rat is the first of the zodiac cycle. In the old days, rats were believed to be the symbol of wealth and luck due to their nature of food seeking. If your birth sign is rat, you are smart and happy.

Level of difficulty: ⭐⭐⭐ What you need: square color paper, marker.

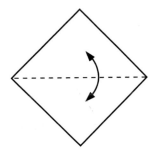

1. Valley fold and unfold to form a crease in the middle.

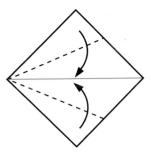

2. Valley fold towards the center.

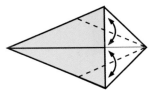

3. Valley fold towards the center and unfold to form a crease.

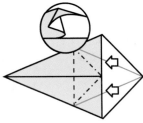

4. Push to open following the open-headed arrow. Then valley and mountain fold.

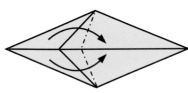

5. Mountain fold the 2 small triangles following the arrows.

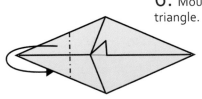

6. Mountain fold the left triangle.

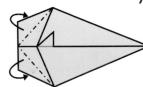

7. Mountain fold.

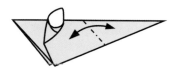

8. Mountain fold the top downwards.

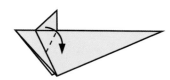

9. Valley fold to the lower right.

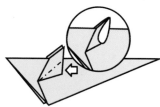

10. Push to open following the open-headed arrow. This is the ear of the rat. Flip over and repeat steps 9 and 10 behind.

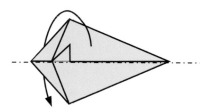

11. Mountain fold and unfold to form a crease.

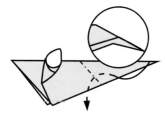

12. Reverse fold following the arrow.

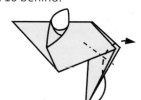

13. Outside reverse fold the bottom tip following the arrow.

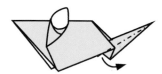

14. Mountain fold both edges.

15. Use your marker to draw the eyes, nose and whiskers of the rat. A little cute rat is done.

02

Ox

Ox is the second of the zodiac cycle. It is honest and hard-working, helping the farmers plow. If your birth sign is ox, you are diligent, steadfast, strong, and perseverant.

Level of difficulty: ★ ★ ★   What you need: square color paper, marker.

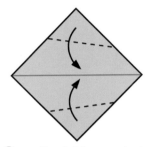

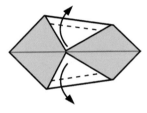

1. Valley fold and unfold to form a crease in the middle.

2. Valley fold towards the center.

3. Valley fold the top and the bottom edges.

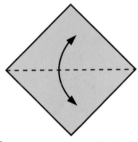

4. Valley fold and unfold to form a crease.

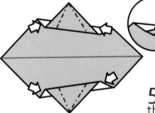

5. Push to open following the open-headed arrows and mountain fold.

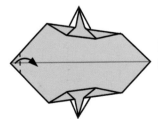

6. Valley fold the left small triangle inwards.

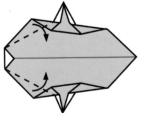

7. Valley fold inwards.

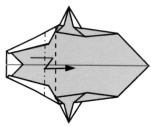 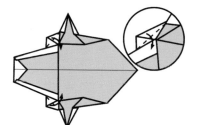 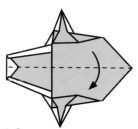

8. Fold along the mountain and valley lines to form a pleat fold.

9. Valley fold inwards.

10. Valley fold the upper portion downwards.

 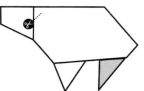

11. Reverse fold following the arrow. This is the hind leg of the ox.

12. Cut along the dashed line.

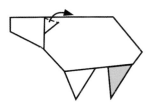 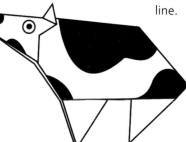

13. Valley fold the cut portion upwards. This is the ear of the ox.

14. Draw the patterns and eyes with your marker. A simple and honest ox is complete.

Tiger

Tiger is the third of the zodiac cycle. Its brave and fierce characters have granted it the King of the Jungle. If your birth sign is tiger, you are enthusiastic and brave.

Level of difficulty: ⭐ ⭐   What you need: square color paper, marker.

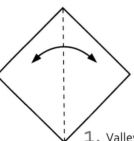

1. Valley fold and unfold to form a crease.

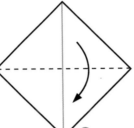

2. Valley fold downwards.

3. Valley fold both sides towards the center.

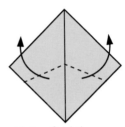

4. Valley fold the 2 bottom triangles upwards. These are the ears of the tiger.

5. Valley fold the 2 triangles on the side towards the center.

6. Valley fold the top triangle downwards.

7. Flip to the right 180°.

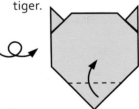

8. There are 2 triangles at the bottom, one in front and one at the back. First is to valley fold the front triangle upwards.

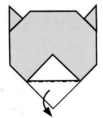

9. Then mountain fold the back triangle.

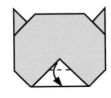

10. Valley fold the little triangle downwards.

11. Draw the patterns and eyes using your marker. A little cute tiger is done.

Rabbit

Rabbit is the fourth of the zodiac cycle. According to the Mid-Autumn Festival folklore, a Jade Rabbit lived in the Moon Palace with Chang'e, the Chinese goddess of the moon. If your birth sign is rabbit, you are gentle, thoughtful and flexible.

Level of difficulty: ⭐⭐   What you need: square color paper, marker.

1. Valley fold and unfold to form a crease.

2. Valley fold towards the center.

3. Valley fold the bottom triangle upwards.

4. Cut along the dashed line in the middle.

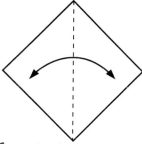

5. Valley fold.

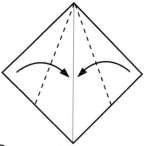

6. Now there are 2 triangles. First is to valley fold the front triangle towards the upper left. This is the ear. Flip to the right 180°.

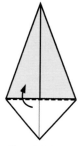

7. Next is to mountain fold the back triangle. This is the other ear. Note that the ears are not parallel. Flip over.

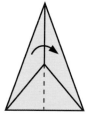

8. Push to open the back and mountain fold the 2 left triangles inwards.

9. Reverse fold the upper triangle.

10. Draw the lips and eyes with your marker. A smiling rabbit is complete.

15

Dragon

Dragon is the fifth of the zodiac cycle. It has four feet and a pair of horns on a snake-like body that is covered by scales. In Chinese culture, dragon has a very high authority and is able to grant people luck. If your birth sign is dragon, you are full of power and courage.

Level of difficulty: ★★★★ What you need: rectangular color paper (width: length = 1:4), marker.

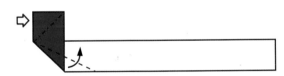

1. Valley fold and unfold to form creases.

2. Mountain fold downwards and valley fold upwards.

3. Reverse fold at mountain line. Then valley fold upwards.

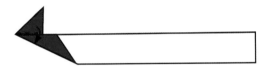

4. Valley fold the top 2 triangles downwards.

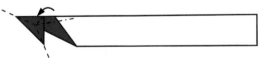

5. Valley and mountain fold to the left.

6. Mountain and valley fold following the arrow to make the dragon muzzle.

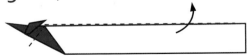

7. Mountain fold the dragon head downwards. Then valley fold and flip the dragon body outwards.

8. Unfold the dragon body following the arrow.

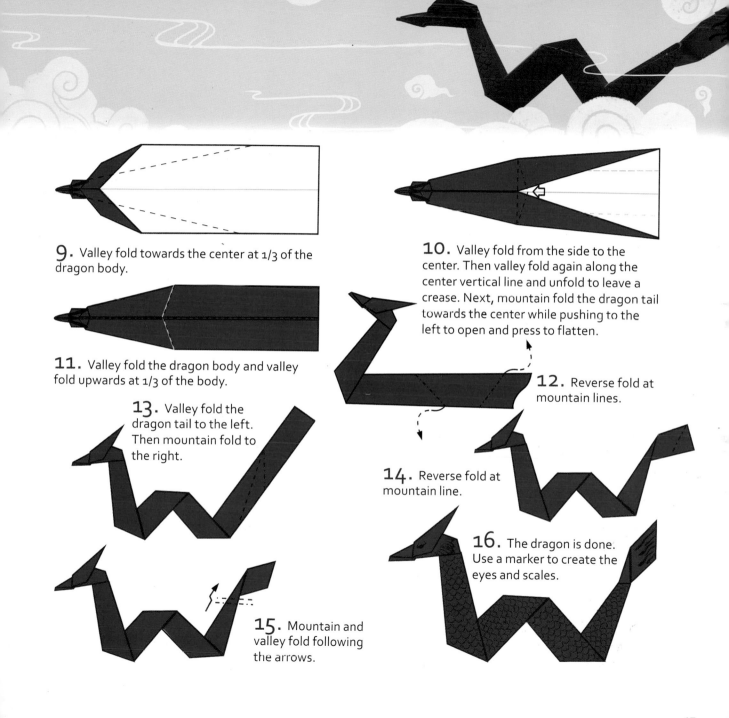

9. Valley fold towards the center at 1/3 of the dragon body.

10. Valley fold from the side to the center. Then valley fold again along the center vertical line and unfold to leave a crease. Next, mountain fold the dragon tail towards the center while pushing to the left to open and press to flatten.

11. Valley fold the dragon body and valley fold upwards at 1/3 of the body.

12. Reverse fold at mountain lines.

13. Valley fold the dragon tail to the left. Then mountain fold to the right.

14. Reverse fold at mountain line.

15. Mountain and valley fold following the arrows.

16. The dragon is done. Use a marker to create the eyes and scales.

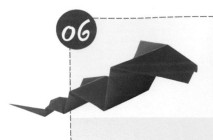

Snake

Snake is the sixth of the zodiac cycle. In Chinese mythology, Nüwa, the Mother Earth, was a goddess with a human body and snake tail. She mended the heavens and blessed the earth. If your birth sign is snake, you are smart, humorous, and calm.

Level of difficulty: ⭐⭐   What you need: square color paper, marker.

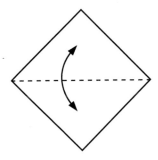
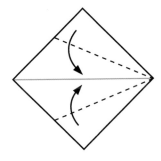

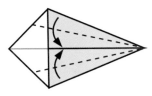

1. Valley fold and unfold to form a crease in the middle.

2. Valley fold towards the center.

3. Valley fold once more towards the center.

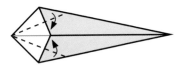
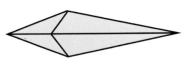

4. Valley fold towards the center.

5. Flip down 180°.

6. Pleat along the valley and mountain lines.

7. Outside reverse fold the left tip.

8. Reverse fold the left tip. This is the snake head.

9. Draw the eyes using your marker. A winding snake is finished.

Horse

Horse is the seventh of the zodiac cycle. It has long legs and short ears. Not only can it gallop at the war zone, but it can also carry us on a journey of thousands of miles. If your birth sign is horse, you are energetic, hard-working, and brave.

Level of difficulty: ⭐⭐⭐⭐   What you need: square color paper, scissors, marker.

1. Valley fold downwards.

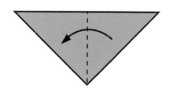

2. Valley fold to the left.

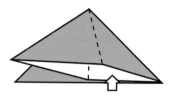

3. Push to open following the open-headed arrow.

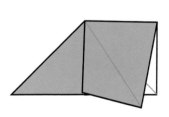

4. Now you get what is shown on the picture. Flip it to the right 180°.

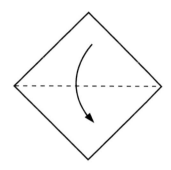

5. Valley and mountain fold and you will get a square.

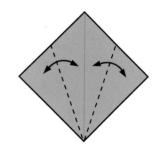

6. Set the open side downwards. Mountain fold towards the center and unfold to form a crease.

7. Open the front diamond. Mountain fold following the arrows and press to flatten it.

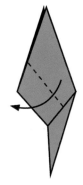

8. Flip to the right 180° and repeat steps 6 and 7.

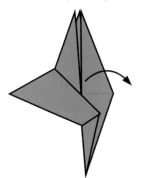

9. Reverse fold the lower right triangle following the arrow. Repeat on the left. Then fold the top triangles downwards.

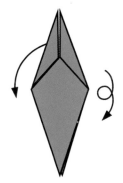

10. Fold the left triangle downwards and flip down 180°.

11. Valley fold towards the lower left.

12. Flip over. Repeat step 11. Fold towards the lower right. Flip over again.

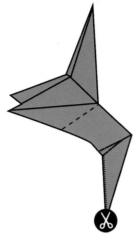

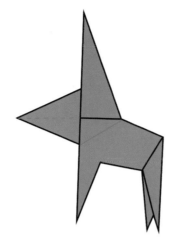

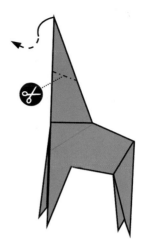

13. Valley fold downwards. This is the foreleg. Cut along the dashed line to create the 2 hind legs.

14. Follow step 13 to fold the diamond shape downwards. This is the other foreleg.

15. Cut along the dashed line. Reverse fold.

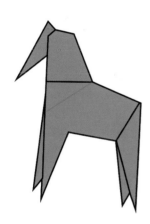

16. This is the head.

17. Reverse fold the muzzle and 4 legs.

18. Use a marker to create the eyes and patterns. The cute little horse is ready.

Ram

Ram is the eighth of the zodiac cycle. It has a pair of spiral shaped horns and is covered by soft hair. With the very meek and mild characters, it never harms anyone. If your birth sign is ram, you are kind and friendly. Everyone likes to be close with you.

Level of Difficulty: ⭐⭐⭐⭐☆ What you need: square color paper, marker.

1. Valley fold at the center and unfold to form a crease. Then valley fold again to the center following the arrows.

2. Mountain fold following the arrows and unfold to form the creases.

3. Push to open following the arrow and press.

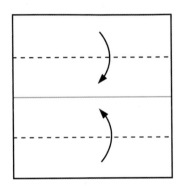

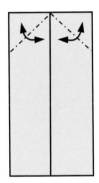

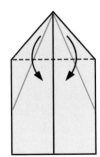

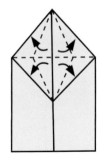

4. Valley fold upwards. Flip to the right 180°.

5. Valley fold towards the center. Unfold to form the creases. Flip to the right 180° again.

6. Valley fold downwards.

7. Valley fold following the arrows.

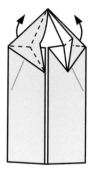 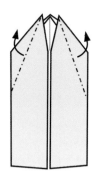 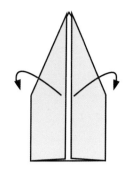 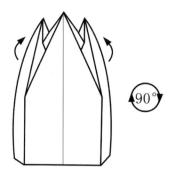

8. Now you can see the triangle flipped over to the right. Repeat on the left side.

9. Mountain fold following the arrows.

10. Open following the arrows.

11. Open following the arrows. Then turn the 2 trapezoids to the back.

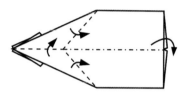

12. Valley fold the tip to the right following the arrows. Mountain fold the right part downwards following the arrow.

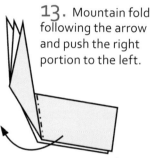

13. Mountain fold following the arrow and push the right portion to the left.

14. Now you get what is shown on the picture. Then valley fold the corner of the first and third layers downwards. These are the horns.

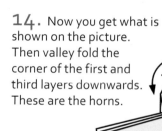

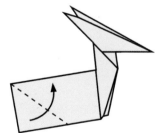 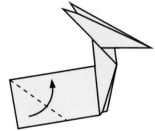 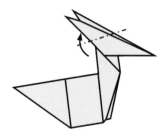

15. Reverse fold following the arrow.

16. Valley fold upwards following the arrow. Repeat behind.

17. Mountain fold downwards following the arrow. This is the horn. Repeat behind.

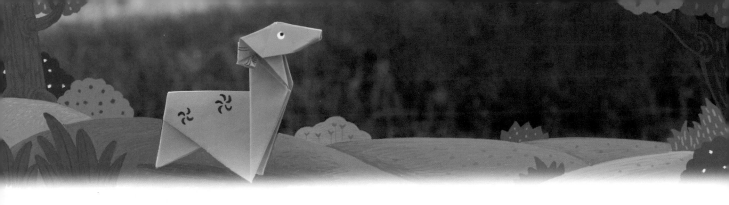

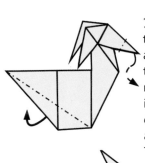

18. Reverse fold the top right triangle along the line following the arrow. This is the muzzle. Mountain fold inwards the lower left corner following the arrow. Repeat behind. This is the tail.

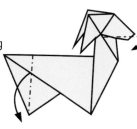

19. Fold down the 2 triangles on the left following the arrow. Then reverse fold the tail. The tail is set. Tuck in the triangle at the muzzle along the line.

20. Mountain fold following the arrow.

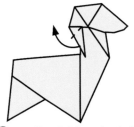

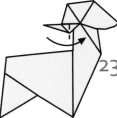

23. Mountain fold to the right.

21. Push in along the mountain line following the arrow.

22. Valley fold to the left.

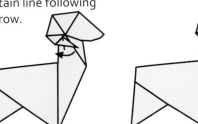

24. Valley fold to the left.

25. Mountain fold to the top right. Repeat on the other side.

26. Draw the eyes. Muzzle and patterns with your marker. A meek and cute ram is complete.

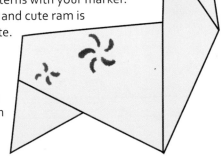

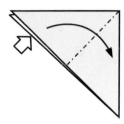

Monkey

Monkey is the ninth of the zodiac cycle. In the very famous Chinese novel *Journey to the West*, Sun Wukong, the Monkey King, is able to travel to the heaven and hell. Knowing 72 transformations with his quick wits and bravery, he is capable of defecting the demons and monsters. If your birth sign is monkey, you are smart and funny.

Level of difficulty: ★★★★ What you need: square color paper, marker, scissors.

1. Valley fold downwards.

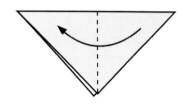

2. Valley fold following the arrow.

3. Squash fold the top triangle following the arrow.

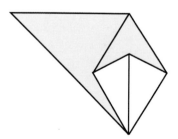

4. Press down the triangle.

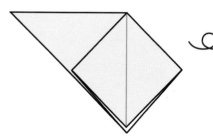

5. Now you get as shown on the picture. Flip to the right 180°.

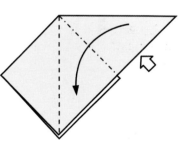

6. Squash fold the triangle following the arrow.

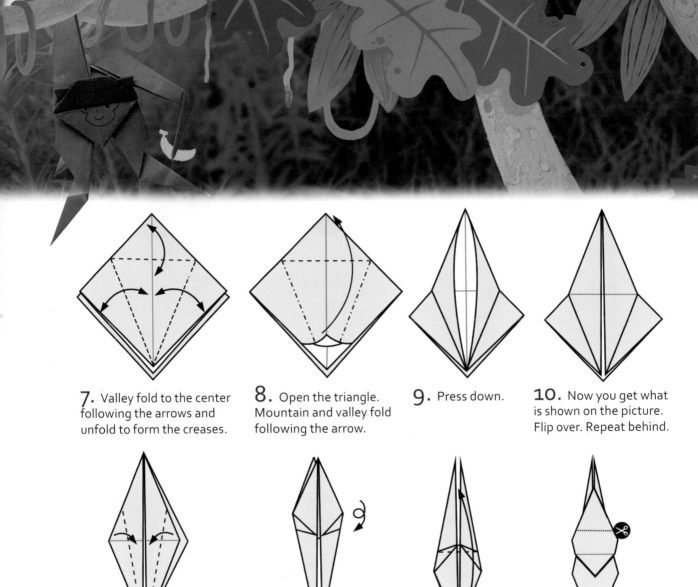

7. Valley fold to the center following the arrows and unfold to form the creases.

8. Open the triangle. Mountain and valley fold following the arrow.

9. Press down.

10. Now you get what is shown on the picture. Flip over. Repeat behind.

11. Valley fold towards the center. Repeat behind.

12. Now you get what is shown. Rotate upside down.

13. Valley fold upwards following the arrow.

14. Cut along the dashed line.

15. Mountain fold following the arrow.

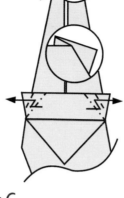

16. Pleat fold following the arrows on both sides. These are the ears.

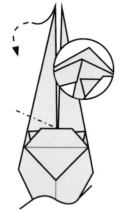

17. Outside reverse fold following the arrow.

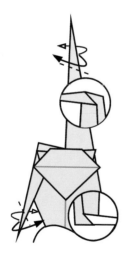

18. Outside reverse fold the 2 arms following the arrows.

19. Reverse fold the upper hand downwards. Cut along the dashed lines below. Mountain fold following the arrows. These are the legs.

20. Use a marker to draw the eyes, mouth and hair. Your monkey is done.

Rooster

Rooster is the tenth of the zodiac cycle. Every morning before sunrise, it stands straight with its head up high to crow aloud, waking people up to start a new day. If your birth sign is rooster, you have a forgiving heart. Helping people can make you joyful.

Level of difficulty: ⭐⭐⭐   What you need: square color paper, marker, scissors.

1. Valley fold and unfold to form a crease.

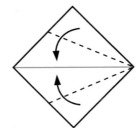

2. Valley fold towards the center following the arrows.

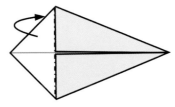

3. Mountain fold the triangle following the arrow.

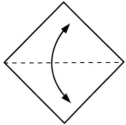

4. Valley fold towards the center following the arrows.

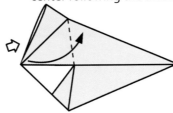

5. Pull the corner outwards following the arrow and valley flod.

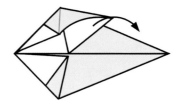

6. Press down. Repeat below.

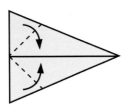

7. Now you get what is shown on the picture. Valley fold to the left.

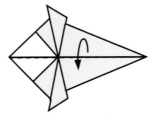

8. Valley fold.

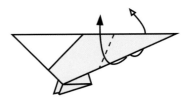

9. Outside reverse fold following the arrows.

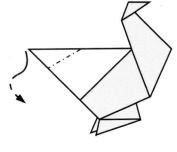

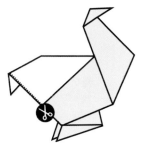

10. Outside reverse fold following the arrows.

11. Reverse fold following the arrow.

12. Cut along the dashed line. Repeat behind.

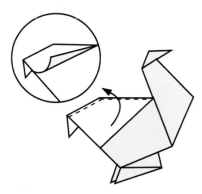

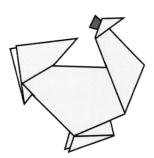

13. Valley fold the cut portion upwards following the arrow. Repeat behind. This is the tail.

14. Cut a small piece of red paper and attach above the head as the comb.

15. Draw the eyes and patterns with your marker. Your rooster is all set.

Dog

Dog is the eleventh of the zodiac cycle. It has a vigorous body, sensitive nose, and big ears. During hot weather, it pants and sticks out its tongue to cool down. Not only is it the guard of our home, but also a true friend of ours. If your birth sign is dog, you are faithful and honest to people around you.

Level of difficulty: What you need: square color paper, marker.

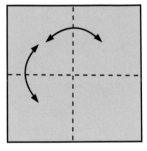

1. Valley fold and unfold to form the creases.

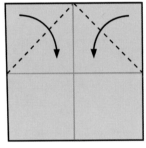

2. Valley fold the 2 upper triangles towards the center.

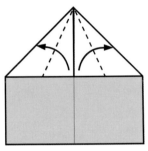

3. Valley fold outwards following the arrows.

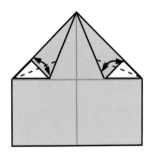

4. Valley fold and unfold to form the creases.

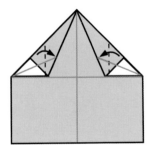

5. Valley fold inwards following the arrows.

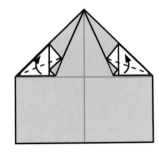

6. Valley fold upwards following the arrows. These are the ears.

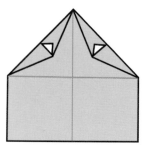

7. Now you get what is shown on the picture. Flip to the right 180°.

8. Valley fold towards the center following the arrows.

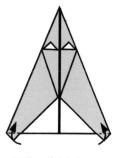

9. Valley fold the 2 small triangles upwards.

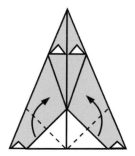

10. Valley fold towards the center following the arrows and tuck the tips inside the triangles above.

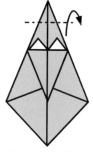

11. Mountain fold the top triangle downwards following the arrow. This is the muzzle.

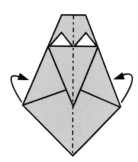

12. Mountain fold.

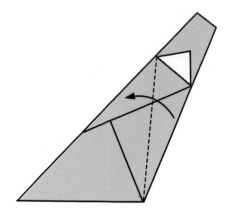

13. Valley fold to the left following the arrow. Repeat behind.

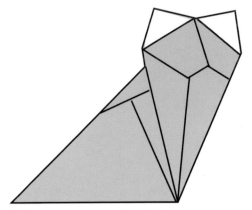

14. Now you get what is shown on the picture.

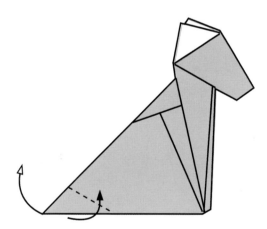

15. Outside reverse fold along the valley line. This is the tail.

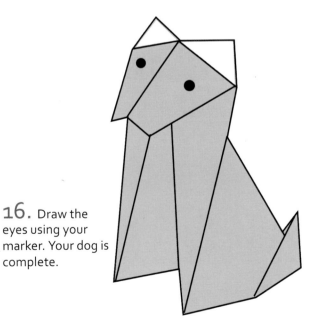

16. Draw the eyes using your marker. Your dog is complete.

Pig

Pig is the last of the zodiac cycle. It has a chubby body, short legs, prominent ears, and upturned nose. Its love of food and snoozes makes it adorable and meek. If your birth sign is pig, you have a lot of interesting friends around.

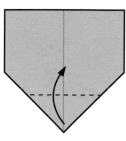

Level of difficulty: What you need: square color paper, marker.

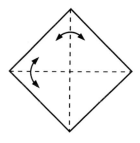

1. Valley fold following the arrows and unfold to form the creases.

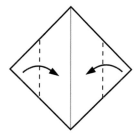

2. Valley fold towards the center.

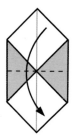

3. Valley fold following the arrow.

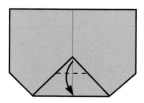

4. Valley fold upwards.

5. Valley fold downwards the tip of the triangle.

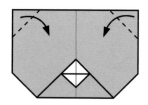

6. Valley fold the 2 top corners towards the center.

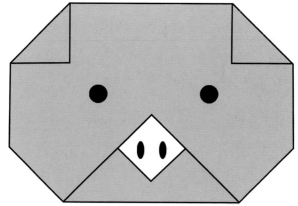

7. Use your marker to draw the eyes and snout. The pig is born.

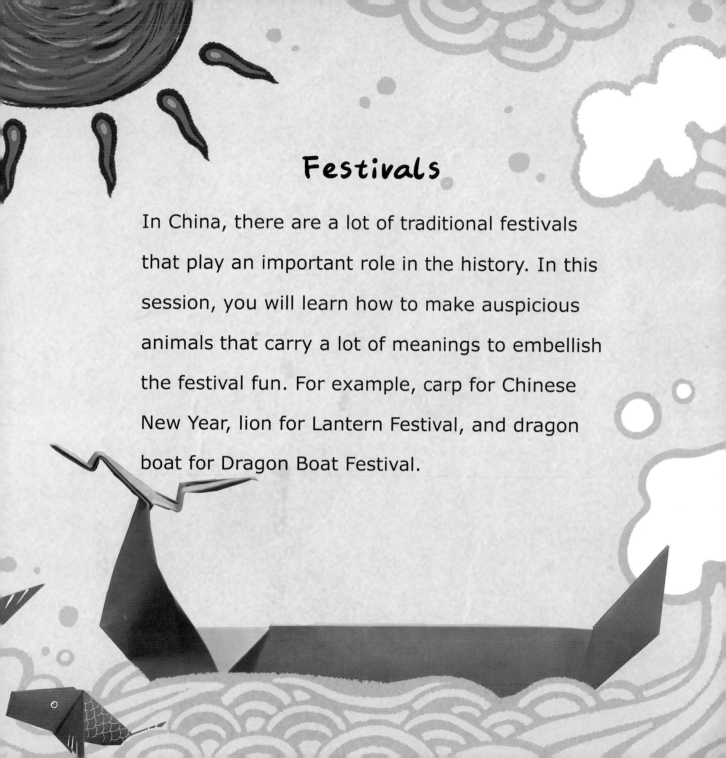

Festivals

In China, there are a lot of traditional festivals that play an important role in the history. In this session, you will learn how to make auspicious animals that carry a lot of meanings to embellish the festival fun. For example, carp for Chinese New Year, lion for Lantern Festival, and dragon boat for Dragon Boat Festival.

Carp

In Chinese, the word "fish" carries a lot of propitious meanings, bringing people fortune. On Chinese New Year, therefore, carps can be found everywhere, such as delicious dishes for the meals, beautiful paper cuttings on the windows, and crafty lanterns in the gardens. The red carps are more rejoicing and bring you good luck.

Level of difficulty: ☆   What you need: square color paper, marker.

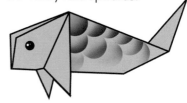

1. Valley fold towards the center.

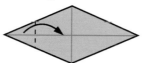

2. Mountain fold following the arrow.

3. Squash fold following the arrows.

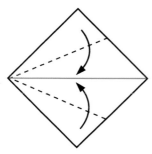

4. Valley fold to the left.

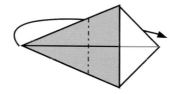

5. Valley fold to the right.

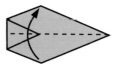

6. Valley fold upwards.

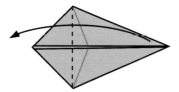

7. Valley fold to the right. This is the pectoral fin. Repeat behind.

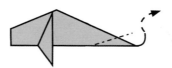

8. Reverse fold following the arrow. This is the caudal fin.

9. Draw the eyes and scales using your marker. The fish is complete.

Lion Head

The lion is coming but don't be afraid! This lion knows how to dance and is very meek and mild. During Chinese New Year, people wear colorful lion costumes, holding a big lion head, and perform the lion dance following the cheerful music. The lion eyes are big and round with long lashes. They are winking at you now!

Level of difficulty: ⭐ ⭐ What you need: square color paper.

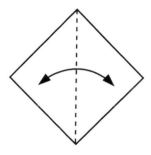

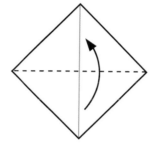

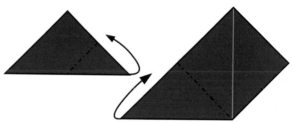

1. Valley fold and unfold to form a crease.

2. Valley fold upwards.

3. Valley fold following the arrow and press down.

4. Valley fold the left triangle.

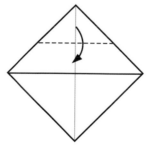

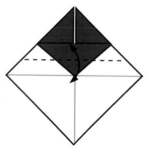

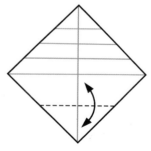

5. Now you get what is shown on the picture. Valley fold the top triangle downwards.

6. Valley fold downwards following the arrow.

7. Valley fold downwards and unfold to leave a crease.

8. Valley fold upwards and unfold to form the crease.

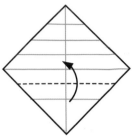

9. Valley fold upwards following the arrow.

10. Valley fold downwards following the arrow.

11. Now you get what is shown on the picture. Repeat steps 9 and 10 on the top triangle.

12. Now you get what is shown. Valley fold downwards.

13. Valley fold upwards following the arrow.

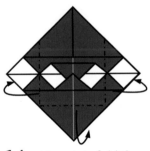

14. Mountain fold the triangles at the bottom and on the sides.

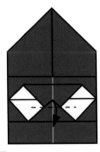

15. Valley fold downwards following the arrow.

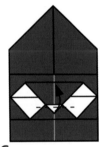

16. Valley fold upwards following the arrow.

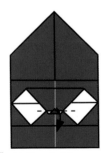

17. Valley fold downwards following the arrow.

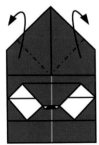

18. Mountain fold the 2 ears to the sides following the arrows.

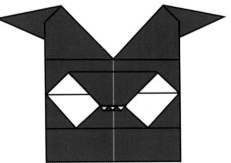

19. The lion head is done.

Dragon Boat

The Dragon Boat Festival is on the fifth day of the fifth month of the lunar calendar. During this festival, friends and families like to get together to share *zongzi* (sticky rice dumplings) and race dragon boats. The dragon boat racing is one of the most favorable sports. Look at the powerful dragon head on the bow and the upturned stern. Let's make a dragon boat and see who can win the race!

Level of difficulty: What you need: rectangular color paper (width: length = 1:4), marker.

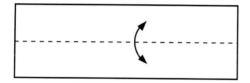

1. Valley fold and unfold to form a crease.

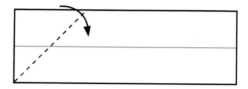

2. Valley fold downwards following the arrow.

3. Valley fold upwards following the arrow.

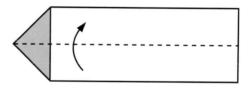

4. Valley fold upwards following the arrow.

5. Now you get what is shown on the picture.

6. Unfold completely showing the creases.

7. Valley fold to the right at the intersection of the creases.

8. Reverse fold the 2 triangles following the arrows.

9. Valley fold and unfold to form the creases.

10. Valley fold towards the center following the arrows. This is the dragon head.

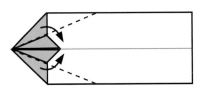

11. Valley fold towards the center and tuck behind the head.

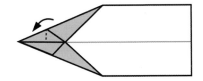

12. Valley fold to the left following the arrow.

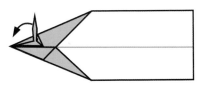

13. The horn is up. Repeat to make the other horn.

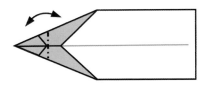

14. Mountain fold and unfold to form a crease.

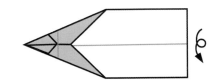

15. Flip down 180°.

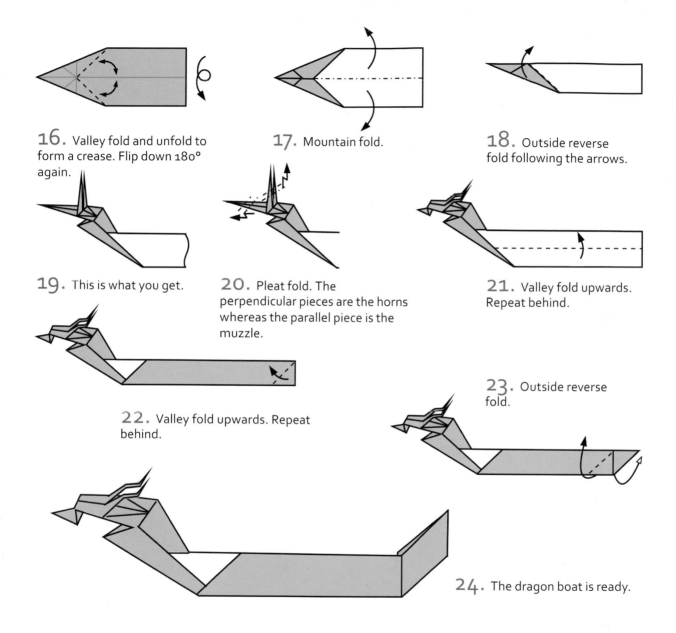

16. Valley fold and unfold to form a crease. Flip down 180° again.

17. Mountain fold.

18. Outside reverse fold following the arrows.

19. This is what you get.

20. Pleat fold. The perpendicular pieces are the horns whereas the parallel piece is the muzzle.

21. Valley fold upwards. Repeat behind.

22. Valley fold upwards. Repeat behind.

23. Outside reverse fold.

24. The dragon boat is ready.

04

Flower Basket

Mother's Day is coming. Let's learn how to make a flower basket for holding roses or carnations and give to your beautiful and hard-working mother!

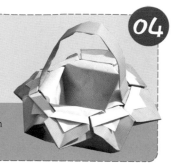

Level of difficulty: ⭐⭐⭐ What you need: 2 square color paper (the color can be different), rectangular color paper, scissors.

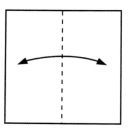

1. Valley fold and unfold to form a crease.

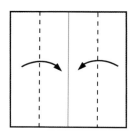

2. Valley fold towards the center.

3. Valley fold and unfold to leave a crease.

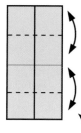

4. Valley fold towards the center and unfold to form the creases.

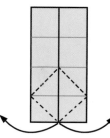

5. Squash fold the bottom half.

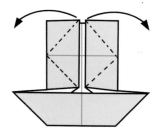

6. Squash fold the top half same as step 5.

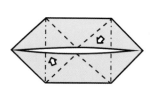

7. Valley and mountain fold. Rotate 45° clockwise.

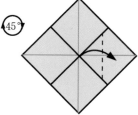

8. Valley fold to the right.

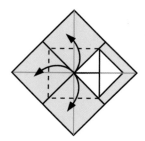

9. Valley fold the other 3 corners as step 8.

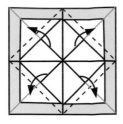

10. Valley fold outwards.

11. Mountain fold the first layer inwards following the arrows.

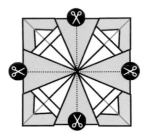

12. Cut along the dashed lines to get 4 basket components.

13. Take another square color paper and repeat steps 1 to 11. Then insert the 4 components from step 12 as shown in the picture.

14. Valley fold following the arrows and insert the corners into the gaps where the red dots are.

15. Push open the basket following the open-headed arrows.

16. Flip over the basket and adjust the base.

17. Cut a long strip for the basket handle and insert into the gaps where the red dots are. Your basket is complete!

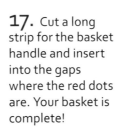

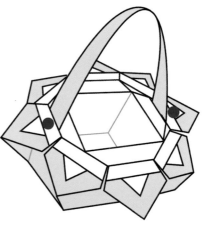

05

Tie

Your father works very hard and this is the way how he shows his love and care. Father's Day is coming. Let's make a stunning tie for him. He will look more handsome when he goes to work with it.

Level of difficulty: ⭐   What you need: square color paper.

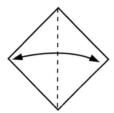

1. Valley fold and unfold to form a crease.

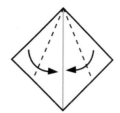

2. Valley fold to the center.

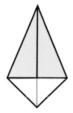

3. Now you get what is shown on the picture. Flip to the right 180°.

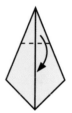

4. Valley fold downwards.

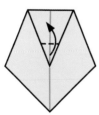

5. Valley fold upwards.

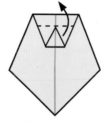

6. Valley fold upwards.

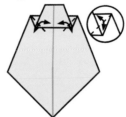

7. Valley fold following the arrows and unfold to form the creases.

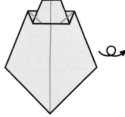

8. Now you get what is shown. Flip over.

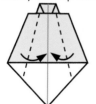

9. Valley fold to the center.

10. Now you get what is shown on the picture. Flip over.

11. Your tie is done!

Blessings

In this session, you will learn how to make butterfly, lotus, bottle gourd, and peach. They all have meaningful implications. Give them to those you love and those who love you as unique blessings.

Butterfly

Butterflies are colorful with a large variety of patterns. They like to dance among the flowers like the beautiful flower fairies. Butterflies and flowers are inseparable, just like you and your friends. Let's make a flower fairy together!

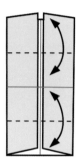

Level of difficulty: What you need: square color paper, marker.

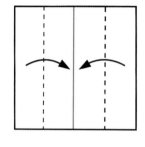

1. Valley fold and unfold to form a crease.

2. Valley fold to the center.

3. Valley fold to the center and unfold to form the creases.

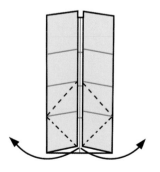

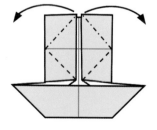

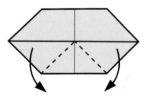

4. Squash fold the bottom part following the arrows.

5. Squash fold the top same as step 4.

6. Valley fold the 2 triangles downwards.

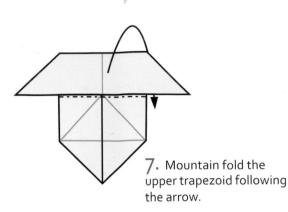

7. Mountain fold the upper trapezoid following the arrow.

8. Valley fold to form 2 triangles following the arrows.

9. Valley fold following the arrow.

10. Reverse fold following the arrow.

11. Spread it. Now you get what is shown on the picture. Flip to the right 180°.

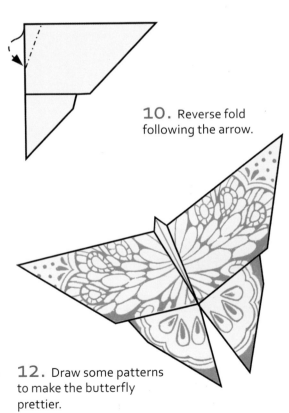

12. Draw some patterns to make the butterfly prettier.

Lotus

In summer time, the pink lotuses floating on the pond are like peachy cheeks of girls, creating a fresh and beautiful scene. The lotus has to break through the dirty mud at the bottom and grow in the sludge, but the lotus exposing above the water yet are clean. Isn't it amazing?

Level of difficulty: ★★★ What you need: square color paper.

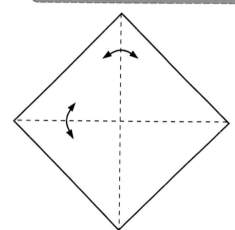

1. Valley fold and unfold to form the creases. The intersection is the center.

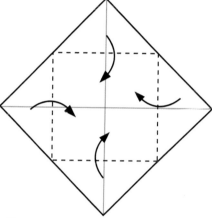

2. Valley fold the 4 corners to the center.

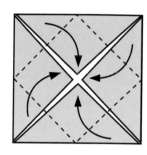

3. Now you get what is shown. Valley fold the 4 corners to the center.

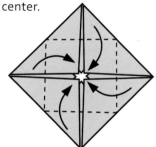

4. The picture shows what you have now. Valley fold the 4 corners to the center.

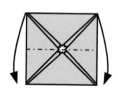

5. Now you get what is shown. Mountain fold downwards following the arrows.

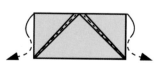

6. Reverse fold the 2 corners following the arrows.

7. Mountain and valley fold and push to the right.

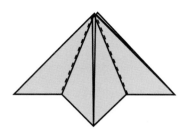 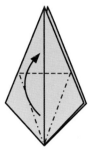 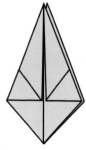

8. Now you get what is shown on the picture. Repeat step 7 on the other 3 sides.

9. The picture shows what you have now. Squash fold following the arrows.

10. Now you get what is shown on the picture. Repeat step 9 on the other 3 sides.

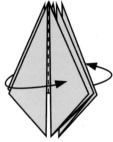 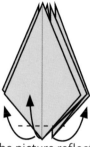 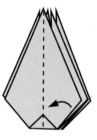

11. Fold the front left triangle to the right and the back right triangle to the left following the arrows.

12. The picture reflects what you have now. Valley fold upwards on the 4 sides following the arrows.

13. Valley fold along the arrow. Repeat on the other 3 sides.

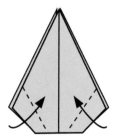  

14. Valley fold along the arrows. Repeat on the other 3 sides.

15. Open the lotus layer by layer and arrange it to form a decent shape. Do not stretch too hard to break the paper.

16. The lotus is complete.

Bottle Gourd

Do you know that bottle gourd has lots of seeds? A seed can then turn into a lot of bottle gourds. In China, bottle gourd hence represents having many descendents. Let's make a plump bottle gourd together!

Level of difficulty: ⭐ What you need: square color paper, marker.

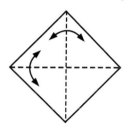
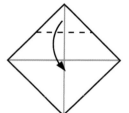
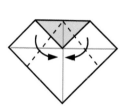
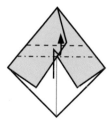
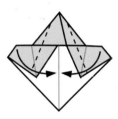

1. Valley fold and unfold to leave the creases. The intersection is the center.

2. Valley fold to the center.

3. Valley fold to the center.

4. Pleat fold from bottom to top to create a trapezoid-like form.

5. Valley fold to the center.

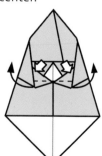
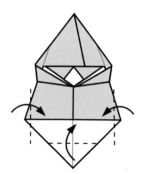
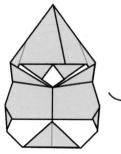
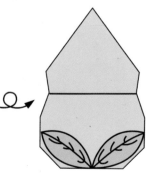

6. Push to open following the open-headed arrows while valley folding.

7. Valley fold following the arrows.

8. See what you get. Flip to the right 180°.

9. Draw a pair of leaves at the bottom. The bottle gourd is done.

Longevity Peach

Pink peaches are juicy and delicious. They have the power of longevity as described in folklore. It is a good idea to give your parents and grandparents a peach on their birthdays to wish them happy, healthy and long life.

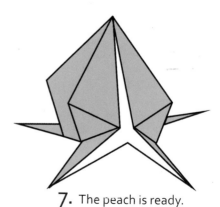

Level of difficulty: What you need: square color paper.

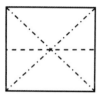

1. Mountain and valley fold.

2. Now you get what is shown. Valley fold to the center.

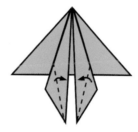

3. Valley fold following the arrows.

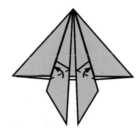

4. Valley fold following the arrows. These are the leaves.

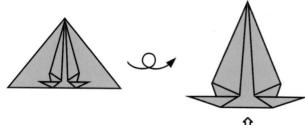

5. This is what you get now. Repeat steps 2 to 4 behind.

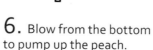

6. Blow from the bottom to pump up the peach.

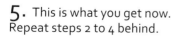

7. The peach is ready.

Chinese Style

Have you ever been to China? If not, that's OK.
You will learn some typical Chinese elements in
this session. Some are Chinese legends and some
can be seen with your own eyes when you visit
China.

Fenghuang

Fenghuang or phoenix is a mythological bird, known to be the king of birds, leading all the birds in the world. It glows with its long train and colorful feathers. You will receive a good luck when you see it!

Level of difficulty: ★★★ What you need: square color paper.

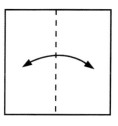

1. Valley fold and unfold to leave a crease.

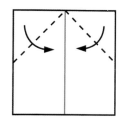

2. Valley fold to the center.

3. Now you get what is shown. Flip to the right 180°.

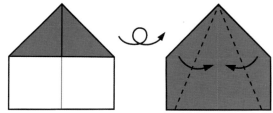

4. Valley fold to the center.

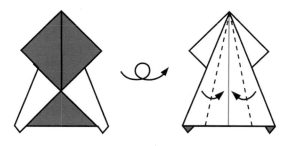

5. Flip out the triangles behind. Flip to the right 180°.

6. Valley fold to the center.

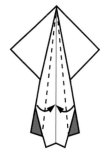

7. Valley fold to the center.

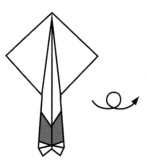

8. This is what you have now. Flip to the right 180°.

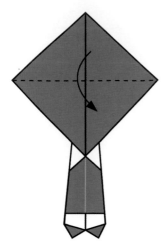

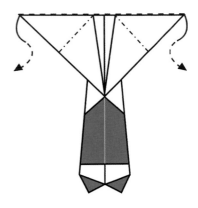

9. Valley fold downwards.

10. Valley fold to the center and unfold to leave the creases.

11. Reverse fold the 2 triangles.

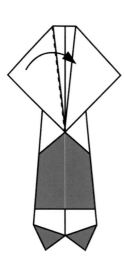

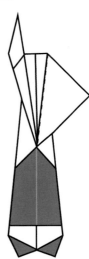

12. Valley fold the top left triangle to the right.

13. Mountain and valley fold following the arrows.

14. The picture shows what you get after pressing. Valley fold to the center.

15. Valley fold to the left.

16. Repeat steps 12 to 15 on the right.

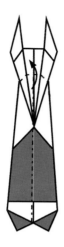

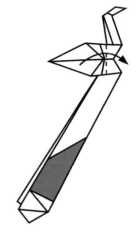

17. Valley fold upwards. Then mountain fold the whole piece.

18. The picture shows the profile. Reverse fold following the arrow. The head is set.

19. Reverse fold. The phoenix body is finished.

20. Valley fold to the right. These are the wings.

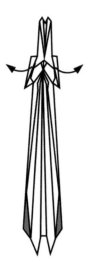

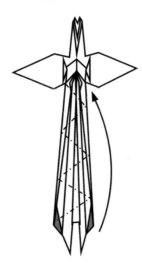

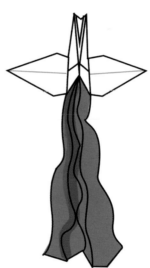

21. Turn the phoenix back up and pull outwards following the arrows.

22. Mountain fold the train.

23. Lay out the train. The phoenix is ready.

Giant Panda

The giant panda is the national treasure of China. It carries only two colors: black and white. It has a big head, big patches around the eyes, and a chubby body. Its favorite food is bamboo.

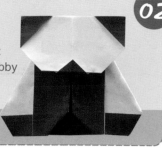

Level of difficulty: ⭐⭐⭐　What you need: square color paper, marker.

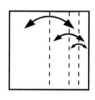

1. Valley fold 3 times and unfold to form the creases.

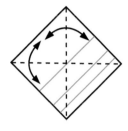

2. Valley fold and unfold to leave the creases.

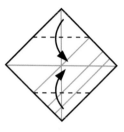

3. Valley fold to the center.

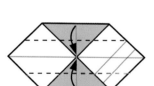

4. Valley fold to the center.

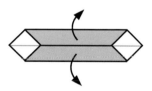

5. Unfold completely to leave the creases.

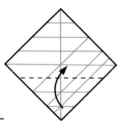

6. Valley fold upwards.

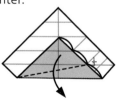

7. Valley fold downwards at 1/3 of the triangle.

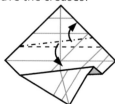

8. Repeat steps 6 and 7 on the upper side.

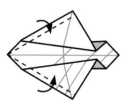

9. Valley fold following the arrows.

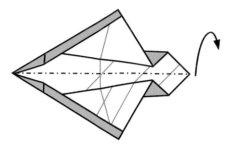

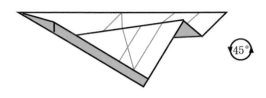

10. Mountain fold following the arrows.

11. The picture shows what you get after folding. Rotate 45° anticlockwise.

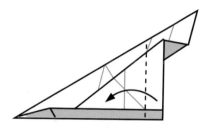

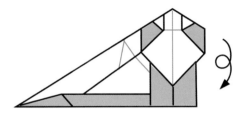

12. Valley fold to the left. Open to set as figure 13.

13. The right is the panda head. Flip down 180°.

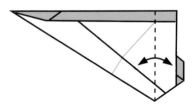

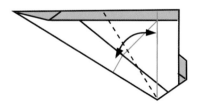

14. Valley fold and unfold to leave a crease.

15. Valley fold and unfold to leave a crease.

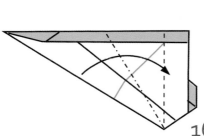

16. Mountain and valley fold to the right following the arrows.

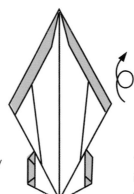

17. Now you get what is shown. Flip down 180°.

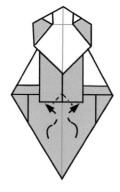

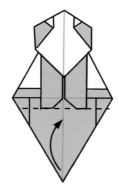

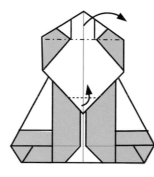

20. Mountain fold following the arrow. Valley fold the bottom of the head upwards.

18. Reverse fold.

19. Valley fold upwards and tuck into the gap.

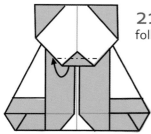

21. Mountain fold following the arrow.

22. Draw the big round eyes with your marker. The panda is ready.

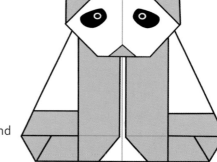

Pagoda

If you come visit China, you may see some very tall pagodas. The shape of every pagoda tier is the same. The higher the tier, the smaller the size. Doesn't it look like the human pyramid in the circus? Construct some pagodas with your friends and see who gets the highest!

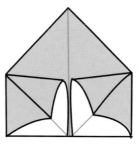

Level of difficulty: ⭐⭐⭐ What you need: 3 square color paper, marker.

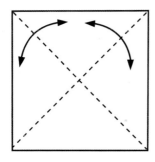

1. Valley fold following the arrows and unfold to form creases.

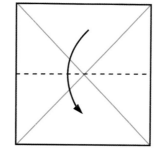

2. Valley fold following the arrow.

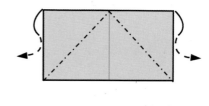

3. Reverse fold.

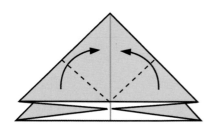

4. Valley fold following the arrow. Repeat behind.

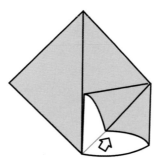

5. Squash fold following the arrow. Press to flatten it.

6. Repeat on the left. Flip over and repeat steps 4 to 5.

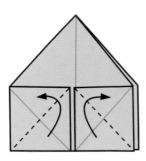

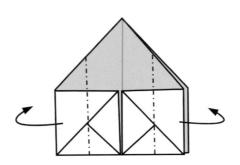

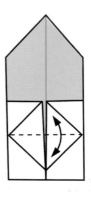

7. Valley fold the front triangles upwards. Repeat behind.

8. Mountain fold inwards following the arrows. Repeat behind.

9. Valley fold the bottom triangle upwards and unfold to form a crease. Repeat behind.

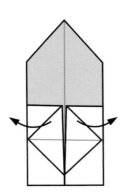

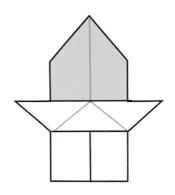

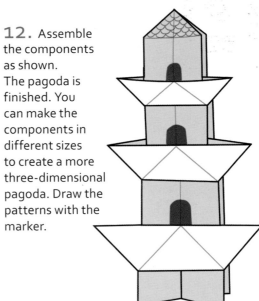

10. Mountain fold and pull out the top triangles. Repeat behind.

11. One of the pagoda components is done. Repeat the above steps to make the other 2 components.

12. Assemble the components as shown. The pagoda is finished. You can make the components in different sizes to create a more three-dimensional pagoda. Draw the patterns with the marker.